A Benjamin Blog
and his Inquisitive Dog
Investigation

Exploring
Rainforests

Anita Ganeri

Raintree is an imprint of Capstone Global Library Limited, a company incorporated in England and Wales having its registered office at 7 Pilgrim Street, London, EC4V 6LB – Registered company number: 6695582

www.raintreepublishers.co.uk
myorders@raintreepublishers.co.uk

Edited by Dan Nunn, Rebecca Rissman, and Helen Cox Cannons
Designed by Joanna Hinton-Malivoire
Original illustrations © Capstone Global Library Ltd
Illustrated by Sernur ISIK
Picture research by Mica Brancic
Originated by Capstone Global Library Ltd
Production by Helen McCreath
Printed and bound in China

ISBN 978 1 406 7107 2
17 16 15 14 13
10 9 8 7 6 5 4 3 2 1

British Library Cataloguing in Publication Data
A full catalogue record for this book is available from the British Library.

Acknowledgements
We would like to thank the following for permission to reproduce photographs: Alamy p. 22 (© John Warburton-Lee Photography); FLPA pp. 9 (Minden Pictures/Kevin Schafer), 15 (Imagebroker/Stefan Huwiler), 20 (Minden Pictures/Chien Lee), 21 (David Hosking), 25 and 29 top (both Silvestre Silva/Holt); Getty Images pp. 10 (Oxford Scientific/Richard Packwood), 24 (Arco Images/Schulz Gerhard; Naturepl.com p. 27 (Anup Shah); Photoshot pp. 11 (© NHPA/Martin Zwick), 19 (© NHPA/Joe McDonald), 23 (© NHPA/Adrian Hepworth); Shutterstock pp. 4 (© Christopher Meder), 5 (© Alexey Stiop), 6 (© Vitaly Titov & Maria Sidelnikova), 8 (© gary yim), 12 (© kkaplin), 13 (© tome213), 14 (© Photogrape), 16 (© Chris Alcock), 17 (© Karen Givens), 18 (© Natali Glado), 26 (© pupunkkop), 29 bottom (© Karen Givens); SuperStock p. 7 (Minden Pictures).

Front cover photograph of a tropical rainforest reproduced with permission of Shutterstock (© Eky Studio).

We would like to thank Michael Bright for his invaluable help in the preparation of this book.

Every effort has been made to contact copyright holders of material reproduced in this book. Any omissions will be rectified in subsequent printings if notice is given to the publisher.

Disclaimer
All the internet addresses (URLs) given in this book were valid at the time of going to press. However, due to the dynamic nature of the internet, some addresses may have changed, or sites may have changed or ceased to exist since publication. While the author and publisher regret any inconvenience this may cause readers, no responsibility for any such changes can be accepted by either the author or the publisher.

Some words are shown in bold, **like this**. You can find out what they mean by looking in the glossary.

Contents

Welcome to the rainforest!

Hello! My name's Benjamin Blog and this is Barko Polo, my **inquisitive** dog. (He's named after the ancient ace explorer **Marco Polo**.) We have just got back from our latest adventure – exploring **tropical** rainforests around the world. We put this book together from some of the blog posts we wrote on the way.

BARKO'S BLOG-TASTIC RAINFOREST FACTS

Tropical rainforests mostly grow in three huge patches: in South America, Africa, and South East Asia. There are also smaller forests in Papua New Guinea and Australia.

Steamy weather

Posted by: Ben Blog | 20 August at 11.03 a.m.

We started our trip in the amazing Amazon rainforest in South America. It's very hot and sticky, and it will be the same tomorrow and the day after that. This is because **tropical** rainforests grow along the **equator**, where it's warm and **humid** all year round.

BARKO'S BLOG-TASTIC RAINFOREST FACTS

It rains almost every day in the rainforest and there are often thunderstorms. I'm already dripping wet. This orang-utan in Borneo is using a leaf as an umbrella.

Spot the rainforest

Posted by: Ben Blog | 9 September at 2.29 p.m.

Our next stop was Rwanda in Central Africa, where we explored this **cloud forest**. It gets its name because it grows high up on the side of a mountain and is often covered in cloud. The Amazon rainforest is called a lowland forest because it grows on low-lying land.

BARKO'S BLOG-TASTIC RAINFOREST FACTS

Parts of a lowland forest sometimes flood when a river rises above its banks. The trees may stay underwater for many months. They make brilliant homes for hungry fish.

Floor to ceiling trees

Posted by: Ben Blog | 26 September at 7.07 a.m.

Staying in Central Africa, we are in the rainforest in Congo. Here on the forest floor, it's so dark and gloomy that it's tricky to get a good snap. The trees above grow in layers, depending on how tall they are. The tallest reach 60 metres (200 feet) – that's eight times as tall as a house.

BARKO'S BLOG-TASTIC RAINFOREST FACTS
The layer below the tallest trees is called the **canopy**. It's like a thick, green roof of leaves and branches. About two-thirds of rainforest animals live in the canopy.

Fabulous flowers

Posted by: Ben Blog | 19 October at 9.42 a.m.

I snapped this enormous flower in Sumatra, South East Asia. It's called a rafflesia, and it measures 1 metre (3 feet) across. Thousands of plants grow in the rainforest because it's so warm and wet. You would not want to get too close to this one, though – it smells of rotten meat!

bromeliad

BARKO'S BLOG-TASTIC RAINFOREST FACTS
Not all rainforest plants grow in soil. Orchids and **bromeliads** grow high up on the branches of trees. They dangle their **roots** in the air to soak up moisture.

This pitcher plant also comes from Sumatra. It looks fabulous, but it's a killer. Its leaves are shaped like a pitcher, or jug, and they are very slippery. When an insect lands on the edge, it loses its footing and falls inside. Then the plant makes juices that **digest** the insect's body.

BARKO'S BLOG-TASTIC RAINFOREST FACTS

Many tall rainforest trees have short roots for sucking goodness from the soil. To stop them falling over, they grow huge extra roots from their trunks. These are called **buttress** roots.

Amazing animals

We headed back to South America to watch some wildlife. I couldn't wait. At least half of all the world's types of animals live in the rainforests. This tiny frog is a poison dart frog. Its bright colours look pretty, but they warn hungry birds that it's deadly poisonous.

BARKO'S BLOG-TASTIC RAINFOREST FACTS
Jaguars are rainforest hunters from South America. They eat deer, tapir, turtles, caimans, and fish. Their teeth and jaws are so strong that they can bite through a turtle's shell. Yikes!

Our next stop was Madagascar, a large island off the coast of Africa. Its rainforests are home to chameleons, and they are amazing animals. They have very long, sticky tongues that they shoot out to catch insects, and big eyes that can swivel nearly all the way round. How useful is that?!

18

BARKO'S BLOG-TASTIC RAINFOREST FACTS

These mountain gorillas live in the **cloud forests** of Central Africa. They spend most of the day looking for food. At night, they sleep in beds they built from branches and leaves.

When I snapped this beauty in Java, Indonesia, I thought it was an orchid flower. Then I looked harder! It's actually an insect, called an orchid mantis. It's the same colour as the orchid, and the flaps on its body look like petals. But, when an insect visits, the mantis snaps it up.

BARKO'S BLOG-TASTIC RAINFOREST FACTS

In the Philippines, huge eagles soar through the tops of the tallest trees. They are looking for flying lemurs or monkeys to eat. They have big, hooked beaks and sharp claws for grabbing their **prey**.

Awesome Amazon

Posted by: Ben Blog | 24 April at 6.07 a.m.

This week, it was back to the Amazon rainforest. It's the world's biggest rainforest – nearly the size of Australia – so there is still plenty to see. The rainforest grows on the banks of the Amazon River, so we are travelling by canoe. Some local rainforest people are coming along as guides.

BARKO'S BLOG-TASTIC RAINFOREST FACTS

Sloths hang upside down from the trees, holding on with their hook-like claws. They spend most of the day fast asleep and only come down to the ground about once a week.

23

Riches of the rainforest

Posted by: Ben Blog | 28 May at 3.33 p.m.

Did you know that lots of everyday things come from the rainforest? They include fruit, spices, chocolate, coffee, and even chewing gum. Many plants make important medicines. This rosy periwinkle from Madagascar is used to treat people with a type of **cancer**.

BARKO'S BLOG-TASTIC RAINFOREST FACTS

Tasty brazil nuts grow on tall trees in the Amazon rainforest. They grow inside huge pods, as big as coconuts. Each nut has a very hard shell, so you need to watch out for your teeth!

Rainforests at risk

Posted by: Ben Blog | 7 June at 5.11 p.m.

All over the world, people are destroying the rainforests. The forests are disappearing so quickly that there may be none left in 50 years' time. Here in Thailand, the forest is being cut down for **timber** and to make space for growing crops. It's a terrible sight.

BARKO'S BLOG-TASTIC RAINFOREST FACTS

These orang-utans in Borneo lost their home when the rainforest was cut down. They were taken to a rescue centre. The centre has a patch of forest that is **protected**, and this is where the orang-utans will live.

Steamy rainforests quiz

If you are planning your own rainforest expedition, you need to be prepared. Find out how much you know about steamy rainforests with our quick quiz.

1. What is the weather like in the rainforest?
a) cold and icy
b) hot, wet, and sticky
c) windy

2. Where does a **cloud forest** grow?
a) on a mountain
b) by a river
c) in the desert

3. How tall are the tallest rainforest trees?
a) 10 metres
b) 150 metres
c) 60 metres

4. Which flower smells of rotten meat?
a) orchid
b) pitcher plant
c) rafflesia

5. Where is the biggest rainforest?
a) Africa
b) South America
c) South East Asia

6. Which of these comes from the rainforest?
a) chewing gum
b) coffee
c) chocolate

7. What is this?

8. What is this?

Answers

1. b
2. a
3. c
4. c
5. b
6. a, b, c
7. brazil nuts in a pod
8. jaguar's coat

29

Glossary

bromeliad plant that grows on tree branches in the rainforest

buttress prop or support

cancer disease that makes people very ill and can kill them

canopy thick roof of treetops over the rainforest

cloud forest rainforest that grows high up on a mountainside and is often covered in cloud

digest break down food into a liquid

equator imaginary line that runs around the middle of Earth

humid damp or moist

inquisitive interested in learning about the world

Marco Polo explorer who lived from about 1254 to 1324. He travelled from Italy to China.

prey animals that are hunted and eaten by other animals

protected saved from harm or damage

root part of a plant that grows into the ground to soak up water and goodness

timber wood used for building

tropical found in warm parts of the world

Find out more

Books

100 Things You Should Know about Extreme Earth, Belinda Gallagher (Miles Kelly, 2009)

Harsh Habitats (Extreme Nature), Anita Ganeri (Raintree, 2013)

Rainforest Animal Adaptions, Lisa Amstutz (Capstone Press, 2012)

Websites

environment.nationalgeographic.com/ environment/habitats
This National Geographic website covers a range of habitats.

www.bbc.co.uk/bitesize/ks2/science/living_ things/plant_animal_habitats/read/1
Learn about habitats on this BBC website.

Index